MICHAL & BATHSHEBA:
DYING IN PLAIN

MICHAL & BATHSHEBA: DYING IN PLAIN

VOLUME ONE: MICHAL

DR. ROYCE M. CARPENTER

proving
press

Book Design & Production:
Columbus Publishing Lab
www.ColumbusPublishingLab.com

Copyright © 2024 by Dr. Royce M. Carpenter

All rights reserved.
This book, or parts thereof, may not be
reproduced in any form without permission.

Cover design by Aaron Richmond, Sr. of Aphografx.

Paperback ISBN: 978-1-63337-909-1
Ebook ISBN: 978-1-63337-783-7
LCCN: 2024905023

Printed in the United States of America
1 3 5 7 9 10 8 6 4 2

*To every person who feels their pain is denied,
ignored, and cast aside,
I SEE YOU!*

INTRODUCTION

A s well-known as the stories of Michal and
Bathsheba are in the Bible, we must wonder if
we really know them? Have we stepped back to
see life from their lens? Are they worthy of coming out
of the shadows? These are the same questions people face
every day in their own lives. People wonder why they are
not seen and what they did to deserve being placed in the
shadows in the first place. Well, it is time we talk about
Michal and Bathsheba and all those who feel broken and
cast aside to let them know they are like beautiful palm
trees that sometimes bend all the way to the ground in
storms. Like a palm that can weather a storm and bounce
back, we must encourage ourselves and others that the
storms of life do not have to keep us down. When we
have no one to talk to, we can talk to God and encourage ourselves while also using tools such as journaling

to strengthen those things that remain in us as we heal from the inside out. Michal and Bathsheba dealt with the dreadful things life sometimes throws our way, but how they handled life made a difference in who they became. Who are you becoming?

1.
A TALE OF TWO WOMEN

On life, we all have myriad experiences that impact our thoughts and behaviors in conscious and unconscious ways. Sometimes we meet people who are kind, but we do not know their stories of traversing tragedy, despair, or heartbreak. Instead, we just see their kindness and pleasant demeanor and enjoy being around them. Other people are mean and angry, and we have no idea why they are that way, either. We do not know that they too have traversed tragedy, despair, or heartbreak, and usually we do not care to find out because their behavior repels us. For example, there are two women in the Bible: Michal, the daughter of King Saul, and Bathsheba, the wife of Uriah the Hittite. Both women had adverse life experiences but reacted differently to their heartbreaks.

I am using the stories of these two women, but their stories could be anyone's story. Their stories both include hurt and pain, but how each woman responded to her suffering impacted her destiny. Whether you have read the Bible or not, these stories transcend religion, culture, time, race, and gender. Their stories are our stories, no matter who we are, where we grew up, or who our parents may be. We all have dealt with hurt and must ask ourselves if we are living rich and mentally free lives, or if we are *dying in plain sight.*

Michal and Bathsheba both married the same man at different times: King David. Michal was the first woman he married, and Bathsheba was the last. The Bible describes King David as a man after God's heart, but he also dealt with lust and a desire for power. Like all of us, David dealt with his humanity in all its frailties. He impacted people's lives in many positive ways, such as fighting alongside his soldiers and defending his people, the Israelites, in countless battles. Still, he negatively impacted the lives of people, such as Michal and Bathsheba. When we consider our identities as individuals, as well as the identities of those around us, we all have to admit that we have within our humanity two sides of the same coin.

The focus of this book is not King David's relationship with God, though that is relevant to our story. Rather, the focus is two of his wives, two women, two human beings, Michal and Bathsheba, and how they experienced life, their struggles, and, ultimately, their choices. I know it may be difficult for some people to focus on the subjects of the story, Michal and Bathsheba, and their lived experiences, due to a desire to defend King David. Please do not get distracted by viewing these women's stories through the lens of King David or ponder why he made the choices that he made. Instead, focus on how Michal and Bathsheba dealt with life, trauma, and decisions (good and bad) when faced with challenges. The issue is not whether King David was indeed a man after God's own heart, or how he managed his kingship. Those are different discussions for other times. David dealt with his own trauma from King Saul, his brothers, and even his father, who did not consider him a son worthy to be a king who was chosen by God as a young man. He was overlooked, as evidenced by his father's decision not to bring him to the prophet Samuel when asked to present all his sons to find the one anointed by God. We know that David experienced hurt and pain in addition to his great triumph as a shepherd boy, a skillful musician, a poet, a military leader, and a king, but he is not the focus of this story. Focus on the stories of the two women often forgotten as the victims and survivors of trauma.

A note on journal prompts:

Journaling can help you process your thoughts, feelings, and say things you may not feel comfortable saying to anyone. If you're new to journaling, consider Michal's reflections. At the end of each chapter is a reflection prompt. Write a reflection (or draw, doodle, create in your way) after reading each chapter. You may need time to process your thoughts and feelings after a chapter, so feel free to go back and journal after you have had time to process. There is no right or wrong time or way to journal.

Consider this prompt, and grab a notebook to journal your thoughts.

Take a few moments to assess how you are feeling after reading chapter one. Describe what memories come to mind about your life, whether painful or pleasant, and jot down your thoughts. Who were your confidants as a child? How did you cope with childhood trauma/issues?

2.
MICHAL'S DIARY: MY LOVE

et's imagine Michal as a young woman traversing life without anyone with whom to share her thoughts. She turns to journaling to express herself. Let's imagine what she may have written along her journey.

JOURNAL ONE:

DEAR DIARY, there is a young man who is now working for my father. His name is David. Oh, my goodness, he is amazing! He is not afraid of anything. I heard he fought a lion and a bear while caring for the sheep in his father's pasture. Can you imagine how brave and strong he must be? We are on different economic levels, I know, but I do not care. David is good to my father, and I love my father. Anyone good to my father is all right with me.

I wish my mom were here! I would love for her to give me some advice about men. I wish I could talk to her about how I feel right now and what I should do about my feelings for David, because I am at a loss on how to handle my thoughts. He was supposed to marry Merab, my sister. I don't know what happened between David and my father, though, because my dad married Merab to someone else. Merab was not interested in David anyway, so she was not upset about not marrying him.

I am always thinking about David. I've been watching him from afar for a while, and he seems like a very good person, but I dare not tell my father how I feel. It is challenging to talk to my father for many reasons. Well, it is difficult for me to talk to him about anything. We are a wealthy family, and I am not sure whether my father would approve of my feelings for David. After all, he chose not to allow my sister to marry David, who is a lowly shepherd. There must have been a reason they did not marry, but I don't know what it was.

JOURNAL TWO

DEAR DIARY, I need some help! I have a lot of self-doubt, I know. I am trying to stop comparing myself to my sister and other people, but I keep having negative thoughts, such as, "Am I as pretty as other young ladies? Is my hair as nice as my sister's hair? Am I smart enough? Could anyone love me? What is the right way to love someone?"

I also worry about my figure; there are so many beautiful young women, and I don't feel like I measure up to them. I try not to think about those things, but the negative thoughts just flood my mind sometimes, and I don't know what to do with them.

Just because I'm the daughter of a king doesn't mean that I have it all together, as most people think. People put me on this unreachable pedestal, and then are shocked when I fall short of THEIR expectations. They do not know that it is often lonely as the king's child, since there is no one to confide in or trust. People either want to be around me because of my father, or they hate me for the same reason without even knowing me. Who can I trust to keep my secrets? No one! So, I am writing to you, my dear diary, to put on paper the words and thoughts I feel in my heart.

At least writing in this diary allows me to say whatever I want without people judging me and looking down their noses at me. I tried to share my thoughts, once, with someone who was supposed to be my friend, but that didn't go well. That person lied about me and betrayed me; now, I do not trust anyone. I learned that the only one I have is me, so I will just express myself on paper and say all the things I wish I could say aloud.

I desire to tell my father how I feel about David directly, but that is not an option. I know my father has discovered how much I adore David because one of his soldiers always catches me looking at David, and they tell my father everything. I guess everyone in our area knows how I feel about David from the gossipers in town. I wish I could talk to my father, and I wish our relationship was different. I would love to tell him everything without the judgment that I know would come, but I cannot.

Please don't get me wrong, I love my father, although I am not sure whether he loves me, since he never shows it. We don't have a picture-perfect relationship, or any relationship, really, at least not the kind that some of my friends have with their parents. Some of my friends can tell their mothers and fathers anything, and their parents help them figure out how to pursue and to attain their hopes and dreams.

Young ladies around my age are often close to their fathers, and they learn how they should relate to men by how they are treated and nurtured by their fathers. Again, though, I don't have that type of relationship with my father. He may love me, but he doesn't show me the care and compassion a daughter would typically get from their father. However, I still love my father dearly.

JOURNAL THREE

DEAR DIARY, it's me again. It's been a while since I wrote in these pages. I apologize for neglecting you, but I am so excited to tell you that my father said I could marry David! Remember, I told you he was supposed to marry Merab, but then my father married her to another man? Do you think David may have doubts or second thoughts about marrying me, since he was supposed to marry my sister? They did not have a relationship—it was an arranged marriage—but you never can tell.

As I said before, fathers should teach their daughters how to be treated by a man. However, since I do not have a strong bond with my father, I'm trying to figure out how to be a wife on my own, without even a mother to guide me and to give me wise advice. Of course, I'm still very, very, very excited that I am going to be Mrs. David! I'm going to be the wife of a great warrior. I have so many beautiful expectations: I want to feel that love that I've always yearned for, and for David to fill the void in my heart left by the lack of love from my father. Well, my Dear Diary, that's all for now. Wish me luck!

Consider this prompt, and grab a notebook to journal your thoughts.

What are the thoughts that come to mind about yourself? Are they uplifting thoughts or self-deprecating thoughts? Take a deep look into the recesses of your heart and mind and journal about your thoughts of you. Consider the relationship you had with your parents or caregivers. How did those relationships contribute to your thoughts about yourself?

NOTHING BUT A PAWN!

ost of the time, when people discuss Michal, the youngest daughter of King Saul, they speak with disdain and righteous indignation. Some say that she was an unworthy, ungrateful, mean wife, and that may be true, but let us dive deeper into the cause of her pain. We know that people who are hurting tend to hurt other people. Pain does not make a person's lashing out acceptable, but their pain can shed light and understanding on the reasons they behave the way that they do and how they need prayer, grace, and possibly a helping hand. You or someone you know may be that hurting person. Just know that you are not alone: there is light for your life if you can take a step out of the dark places of your mind.

As we look at Michal, there is nothing shared with us about her mother other than her name, Ahinoam, which means "pleasant." We must wonder, was her mother around during her formative years, or when she became an adult? Did she have any motherly conversations to help direct her along life's road? Did her mother pass away and leave her without a woman to be a guiding light? These are questions we do not know the answers to, yet we often judge Michal, as we do others around us, without knowing the entire mosaic of their life experiences.

Michal's father, King Saul, was the first King of Israel. Even though he was tall, handsome, and from a wealthy family, he dealt with his own issues, such as insecurity. He felt that he was from a tribe that was not important enough to produce a king, and he did not understand why he was chosen. When it was time for Saul to be presented as king, he was found hiding. As far as we are aware, he never addressed these issues. Even after Saul finally accepted the throne and his place in the kingdom was well established, he was still insecure and jealous.

How might Michal's father's insecurity have impacted her life and decision-making process? Did she learn that insecurity and jealousy were normal feelings to embrace? Insecurities impact the way in which people behave, think, and see themselves and others. Insecurity can also cause people to feel anxiety, make unnecessary comparisons between themselves and others, and create unhealthy rabbit holes in their minds.

We all must assess and acknowledge how we feel and how we view ourselves. It is important to discover and to evaluate the reasons that make you feel insecure, the place those feelings came from, and the way in which you will rid yourself of those negative self-judgments and learn how to love yourself. The way in which you love or do not love yourself impacts every relationship in your life, especially the relationship that matters the most. That is, of course, the relationship you have with yourself.

Doing a self-inventory and examining your thoughts and emotions is crucial to achieve lasting peace and security. For example, can you recognize how your insecurities arise while someone else is being praised? Does the praise of others bother you, make you feel small, or seem to threaten your place in the world? Do you unnecessarily compare yourself to others? These are the issues that arose for King Saul in his relationship with David, and they destroyed him. Comparison is a killer of the soul!

David was a young man when he met King Saul. He was a shepherd boy who grew into a warrior in King Saul's army. When David received accolades for his performance in a particular battle, King Saul's insecurities from when he was a young man of insignificance resurfaced, and he began to feel threatened by David. There was nothing that David did or said to King Saul that caused him to feel threatened. The threat arose from within King Saul, though he did not recognize it as such.

From that day forward, King Saul made David an enemy, all because of a threat created within his own mind. Think about your life, work, family, friends, co-workers, and acquaintances. What self-sabotaging threats have you created within your mind?

Eventually, King Saul's insecurities became so prominent that he sought a way to kill David. He first offered his oldest daughter, Merab, to David in marriage. David was a lowly farmer before he joined King Saul's army, and since he was not from a wealthy family, he was forced to offer something other than money as a bride gift. He was a skilled warrior, so he offered his services as a soldier instead of the customary financial payment. After David had risked his life, however, King Saul revoked his promise to give Merab to David in marriage. Instead, he married her to someone else who was a man of noble birth, revealing his lack of respect for David's humble background.

When someone has low self-worth, making others look or feel bad is one method they may use to pump themselves up, though the feeling does not last. It is only a temporary fix to the deeper problem of insecurity and low self-esteem.

King Saul did not stop with this humiliation of David, however, but continued to plot to destroy him.

King Saul knew that his younger daughter, Michal, was intrigued by and in love with David, so he decided to use her as a pawn in his plot to kill David. The king arranged for her to marry David, after he had fought and killed two hundred of King Saul's enemies. Michal became a consolation prize in her father's plan, since his older daughter had already been married to someone else. Michal is the only woman in the Bible described as loving the man with whom her marriage was arranged, making her ultimate heartbreak even more tragic.

Now, imagine your father offering you, his child, up to someone he hated and wished were dead while knowing that you were madly in love with that person. *Dying in plain sight!* Michal's father was not thinking about his lovely daughter who came from his own loins. The king's daughter, like any daughter, should have been protected and nourished. Her father should have been an example of how she should be loved and respectfully treated by a man. Unfortunately, King Saul did the opposite, and this choice undoubtedly increased Michal's feelings of unworthiness and caused the impetus for her heartbreak and long-term bitterness. That is what King Saul, a father, did to Michal, his daughter.

Someone may be reading this book and protesting that in the culture of those days, it was normal to offer daughters in marriage for political means. While that is true, King Saul was a jealous man, and he *hated* David. He was not trying to gain anything from David, a shepherd boy, by giving his daughter to David in marriage; rather, he was trying to kill someone he had established as a rival within his own mind by using his child.

Michal knew that her father hated the man she loved, however, to the point that one night, she risked her own life and defied her father to ensure that David was not killed.

Consider this prompt, and grab a notebook to journal your thoughts.

How has the way you see yourself impacted your relationships with family, friends, coworkers, and acquaintances? Do you have healthy relationships, or do you struggle to maintain nourishing relationships? What self-sabotaging threats have you created within your mind?

4.
MICHAL'S DIARY: MY HURT

JOURNAL FOUR

DEAR DIARY, when David and I first got married, I thought the marriage would change my life. I thought that I would no longer feel loneliness, emptiness, or fear. I thought that my husband would love me, comfort me, and make me feel whole. I thought that my family would grow larger and happier in my husband's presence. All the things that I thought, expected, and anticipated, however, turned out to be figments of my imagination.

David is not mean to me, but he is not the doting husband that I dreamed he would be. Even though I love him with all my heart, I do not think he does, or ever will, love me like I love him.

My father arranged my marriage, but he detests my husband. Why would he arrange for me to marry

someone he despises? My father has always been a little cold toward me, but I never realized that he hated me! Why else would he offer my hand in marriage to someone he views as his mortal enemy, knowing that I love him? I feel like a piece of me is dying every day! My life has been turned upside down. I don't know what to do. My father abhors my husband, though I do not understand why, and he will not tell me.

He even wants me to betray my own husband and set him up to be killed! How could I possibly do something so horrible? Why is my dad asking me to do such a thing? I can't do it; I won't do it! Many people talk about their in-law experiences in horrific ways, but this is beyond words, and it is *my* father who is being crazy, mean, and vindictive. He knows that David loves him and would never do anything to hurt him, so why would he want me to cause the destruction of my own husband? THIS IS CRAZY!

If I do not do what my father asks, he will probably cut me off from being his daughter, remove me from his will, or kill me, but I do not care. I am not sending my husband to his death even if he does not *yet* love me as much as I love him. Aren't I supposed to support my husband through good times and bad times? I left my father's house to marry the man I love and to support him all the days of my life. I did not marry him to allow my father to use me to try to destroy him. I do not know what my father will do to me, but one thing I know is that I am not giving up on my husband!

JOURNAL FIVE

DEAR DIARY, last night I helped my husband escape. I figured out something to say to my father's forces when they came looking for David. I am hurt, confused, and still as lonely as I ever have been, but I know that when David is safe and settles somewhere, he will send for me, and I will gladly join him. Arranged marriage is a common occurrence where I am from, and I have seen how love has grown in many couples over time.

Now that David sees that I will always support him no matter what, I hope that he will understand how much I love him. We can use my support and love as a foundation for him to grow to love me in return. I am so worried about him, but I know that he is skilled at taking care of himself, and he has some strong and capable men with him, so he is not alone. He and my brother are best friends, and I am sure that he will send a note to my brother for me. I am waiting with bated breath to get word that my love is safe.

Consider this prompt, and grab a notebook to journal your thoughts.

Have you ever loved someone who did not love you back equally? Have you ever been disappointed by someone's actions—like Michal was over her father's hatred of her husband—and you felt stuck in the middle? How did that feel? What choices did you feel you had?

5.
MICHAL THE MISUNDERSTOOD

any writers and preachers have crucified Michal for choosing her husband's life over her father's wishes even though she was in a no-win situation. No mercy or thought is ever given to the challenging position in which she was placed by her father. No one cares that she was *dying in plain sight!*

The fact that the times were different does not mean that Michal, a human being, didn't feel hurt, fear, or betrayal by her father. She may have thought that she was not loved as much as her sister because of the juxtaposition of her father's choices of husbands for them. Have you ever felt the sting of the perception that your parent or parents love one or more of your siblings more than they love you? Michal may have started to deal with some unhealthy social comparison issues, which later negatively impacted her relationship with her husband, King David.

Maybe you too have felt neglected by an absent parent, a parent who did not see you for who you are or notice your need for their love and guidance. Like King Saul, your parents may have lived through hurt and had no love to give.

For others, their parent or parents were not in their lives at all, and they were left to wonder, "What is wrong with me?" "Why did they give me away?" "What did I do to make them not love me?"

Even some people whose parents were physically present throughout their childhoods may have felt emotionally abandoned. Your father or mother may have been abusive, cold, and unloving. You may have traversed the world mentally on your own and had to learn life by trial and error, making you feel lonely and bitter. You may want to be more loving, but you are stuck in your past trauma.

Some of you reading this book may have loving parents but were broken by unloving spouses, partners, or friends. The person that you thought would one day be your partner in life, business, or ministry has instead left you alone, broken, and in despair. The person that, you thought would share your most intimate secrets has betrayed that trust, leaving you without a friend and **dying in plain sight!**

Most often, people do not know or understand the history of where bitter behavior originates, and furthermore, they do not care because the ugliness of the bitterness repels them. They only see the remnant of your pain through your negative attitude or behavior.

What about those with a father in their home, a roof over their head, and money in their pockets? What about that child of a CEO, the child of a pastor of a thriving church, synagogue, or mosque, or the child from a loving, two-parent home? There is a notion that they have no "right" to complain, to be lonely, or to feel bitterness because they have the best of everything. Despite what we may think, money does not buy love, and you cannot know what goes on in someone's home. Money does not fill the void of a parent who is always working and striving to make a better life for their family but forgets about the need their child has just to be held or the importance of spending time together. The idea that someone with parents in the home or plenty of wealth has no right to feel pain or loneliness is common, and that is what Michal experienced. Not being aware of what happens in other people's lives behind closed doors can leave us in the dark about what caused their hearts to grow cold.

There are also people in loveless relationships like Michal who cannot understand why the love of their spouse is now cold. They ask themselves what they did to cause the other not to love them anymore. Is it because they put on some weight? Does their spouse have someone else? Is their spouse ashamed or embarrassed by them? They wish their spouse would just tell them what it is so they could fix it! Let us take a deeper look into Michal's pain.

Consider this prompt, and grab a notebook to journal your thoughts.

How do you deal with thoughts of comparison that may pop into your mind? Comparisons to other people's beauty, intellect, or wealth? What do you do to rid your mind of negative comparison thoughts, or do you embrace them and let them grow? If you feel broken, can you recognize where and when the brokenness was birthed?

6.
OH, THE AGONY OF
A MISSED LOVE!

avid was thrilled to be in the service of a king chosen by God. As you may have surmised, Michal married David with the expectation of a great marriage because she loved him and was excited to wed him. Yet she was entering the marriage broken, used by her father because of his insecurities, and betrothed to a man who never expressed genuine love for her. She probably also inherited some insecurity issues from her father. Michal was only the king's daughter, a prize for David, but regardless of how he felt about her at that time, she loved him still.

One night, her father sent soldiers to her home to kill her husband, but she warned him of his impending doom and helped him to escape. She lied to her father's soldiers, meaning that she lied to her father and could have faced death for her betrayal.

What did she get in return for her loyalty to David? *Nothing!* David left. He didn't say "thank you" or "I love you," leave a note, or say that he would send for her, he just left. I know you may be thinking that he was on the run, and yes, he was. However, he found time to meet with her brother, his best friend, to say goodbye, and he arranged for his parents to be moved for their safety. Although Michal had just betrayed her father, her safety was not one of David's priorities. Her life meant nothing to him. She was **dying in plain sight!**

Has someone ever walked out of your life without giving you any explanation? Did you blame yourself, thinking that if you were only attractive enough, made more money, or said all the right things, then they would still be there? If so, their wrong was somehow turned on you by family, friends, or even strangers.

While David was on the run, he married two more wives, and during the entire time of their separation, Michal did not receive a card, note, or message of any kind from her husband. I do not know about you, but sometimes, it seems like the people for whom we do the most are the ones who are the least thankful. Michal almost gave her life for David, yet she was left alone without hearing a word about his safety. Can you imagine how scared she must have been for him? Wondering what was happening to her husband, her love. Anticipating a message for her to join him, no matter where they needed to go. She was in love, and the possibility of death did not deter her from loving him or putting his wellbeing above her own.

Have you ever been so in love that you did not care what people thought of the person or what they said about the relationship? Imagine holding onto that feeling, only to eventually realize that it was unrequited. Michal was already lacking her father's love when she began to realize that David did not love her either, but only used her then left her. She was becoming bitter, not better, and **dying in plain sight!**

What do you do when your life gets turned upside down and you feel all alone, or when there is no one there to help you pick up the pieces of your broken life? What do you do when your constant companion is heartbreak?

Well, it looked as if Michal's life was finally turning around for the better. Quite some time after David had fled from King Saul, Michal's father gave her in marriage once again, this time to a man named Paltiel, a man that loved her wholeheartedly. She was the apple of his eye. Even though biblical researchers report that they never consummated the marriage, Paltiel loved Michal dearly. Michal had never received love, either from her father or from her first husband, David, the man whom she had loved unreservedly but unrequitedly, but now she was finally loved! Imagine how she had battled with low self-esteem, abandonment issues, and unchecked bitterness, finally to find someone who saw her in all her beauty, even with her flaws. A person she thought could melt away all the ugliness in her life, mend her broken heart, and be her life partner.

As you may know or have guessed, however, Michal's fairytale did not have a happy ending. Her father and her brother, David's best friend, died in battle. Just when she thought that she was free and no longer a pawn, she found out that she was wrong. **Dying in plain sight!**

Consider this prompt, and grab a notebook to journal your thoughts.

How do you deal with the unthankful or ungrateful people in your life? Do you continue to cater to them to keep them nearby? Do you block everyone out of your life so as not to feel the hurt that you have experienced by the few ungrateful people you have encountered?

BITTERNESS AND INSECURITY: UNINVITED FRIENDS

David, now King David, wanted to establish himself as ruler, and what better way to do it than to exert your authority by taking back the defeated king's daughter? King Saul was dead, and new alliances were made. David ordered Michal to return to his kingdom, not because he was in love with her, but to assert his dominance.

Michal was once again a pawn being ripped away from the only man who truly loved her. She was forced back to a man she had not heard from or spoken to, not in days but in years, since she had risked her life to help him escape. Her husband, Paltiel, wept at the loss of his love, his friend, his wife. He followed behind Michal, sobbing, as her cousin forced her to leave. Paltiel risked his life to let her know how much he loved her. No one had risked anything for her before, ever. She had always taken the risk, always cared for others, and now she was losing everything and more, all over again. **Dying in plain sight!**

Someone reading this book may have felt that same sense of loss and devastation. Maybe you loved a spouse, and after giving them all you had, they walked away and left you for someone else. Maybe they died, and you were left all alone without a dime. Perhaps you prayed and prayed for a child, and after feeling blessed with conception, the child died in your womb or from senseless gun violence. Perhaps you had a friend to whom you thought you could tell your innermost secrets without judgement, only to be terribly wrong and find yourself brokenhearted. You may have tried to reconnect with a parent who gave you away, or who was in your life, but in an unhealthy way. The reconnection was another disappointing experience and started you on a constant diet of unhealthy pain.

Michal was feeding on pain, heartache, devastation, and despair. What do you do when misery becomes your closest friend? What do you do when you are given to drink from the brook of agony?

No human can fill the empty places in your heart and soul. God is the only one who will never leave you or forsake you. Michal did not turn to God, though; she turned within, to her old friends, bitterness and insecurity. Bitterness and insecurity were the ones with whom she had grown up when she was overlooked by her father. Bitterness and insecurity were the friends on whom she had depended while waiting for her husband David to love her, and later, to send for her. Bitterness and insecurity were the friends with whom she became reacquainted when she was ripped from the loving arms of the only man who ever cared for her. Yes, bitterness and insecurity became the foundation on which she walked and the glass through which she looked.

Therefore, when David brought back the Ark of the Covenant, which represented God's presence, Michal's bitterness and insecurity blinded her from the Lord's love and healing power, which could have mended her heart and soul. Bitterness and insecurity will kill you from within. They rob you of self-love, abundant life, and joy.

David was dancing and praising the Lord as he brought the Ark of the Covenant back to the Israelite people, but Michal was furious and scolded him for his public behavior. She thought of the way he had used her, abandoned her, and discarded her with ease, only to return with two more wives!

He left her in danger for her life but found the time and energy to marry two other women without giving Michal another thought. Then he came home, dancing and seemingly frolicking in front of even more women, embarrassing her yet again. Michal's bitterness and insecurity led her to believe that he was showing off for the women in the town as he returned, instead of viewing his behavior as honest praise to his God. Bitterness and insecurity were her counselors that day.

Please remember that this man had wronged her repeatedly until she became mad and mean. No one acknowledged her pain. No prophet came to give her a healing word. No family member consoled her for any of the losses she had experienced. No friend came to hold her hand. She was alone and in deep despair. She had been **dying in plain sight** for decades, and no one recognized it.

Consider this prompt, and grab a notebook to journal your thoughts.

Are you always the caregiver and never the one being cared for? What do you do to put yourself first? What self-care regimen have you established for your life? Are you feeding on a diet of bitterness and insecurity?

8.
MICHAL: A WOMAN SCORNED

JOURNAL SIX

DEAR DIARY, Paltiel, Paltiel, my dear, beautiful Paltiel truly loved me. He knew I was a mess who had been hurt by so many, but he never used that against me. He didn't ask a thousand questions about why my father had offered him my hand in marriage after I had been married to "the great warrior, David." Paltiel never tried to make me change who I was; he just loved me, even though he realized that I had no more love to give in return.

Now, after being ripped from the one person who truly valued me, I have been torn from his loving arms and brought back to this cold palace. For a millisecond, I had thought that I was called back because David realized how much he missed me and wanted to reconnect since my father was gone. I soon understood that it was not so.

Did you know that this man had the unmitigated gall to force me back from being with the man who loves me, and ONLY me, to return to him, who now has not only one but two more wives! Who does that? Only a selfish son of a gun with not an ounce of respect, care, or compassion for the person who saved his raggedy life! How dare he behave as if he owns me, like I am a piece of furniture he found on the side of the road. He was a lowly farmer until my father plucked him out of obscurity. The fact that my father is gone doesn't make him of royal birth—he is still an uncultured neanderthal. I am so mad, I can't see straight! I bet these two women both think they are somehow the "one." Little do they know, David is out for David. They are probably more trophies, people to use and discard.

Look at him now, coming back into town, dancing with few clothes on in front of the women in the square. I bet his two new wives didn't think that he was going to be courting the ladies so soon. I can't stop crying, and I do not know why. I do not love him anymore, and since he never loved me, I should not be this upset, but I think it is because I am so mad. He should not be allowed to treat people like garbage and get away with it. I mean, I almost DIED for him! I went against my own FATHER for him! What does he do for me? He takes me away from love, the only love I have ever known. This is not fair! He gets to live, to be happy, and to marry again while I am supposed to suffer in silence. Well, forget that! Wait until he gets a little closer, I am going to give him a piece of my mind!

David! Look at you, KING DAVID, galloping around in front of the ladies. The two new wives you brought home aren't enough to satisfy your arrogance. Are you already back out looking for love in all the wrong places? How shameful you look, but I guess that is what you get from someone whose education was tending sheep. No self-respecting king with a proper upbringing would behave as you are right now!

SOMEONE READING THIS might be feeling the same bitter, insecure feelings that Michal was most likely feeling. People blame you and shake their fingers at you, not knowing what you have lived through. They don't realize that your husband has a wandering eye, and that every time you forgive him, he turns around and has another woman on the side. People don't know the molestation you have experienced, or they do not believe that it even happened. They do not know that as the First Lady of the church, you must deal with disrespectful women who feel like they have a right to the pastor, your husband, all day and night with no regard or respect for you.

Perhaps you are the child of a CEO of a Fortune 500 company, and you feel like you are back in the Old

Testament days because your parent wants you to marry someone to solidify a merger that will send your stocks soaring, never considering what you want or that you do not love the person. Perhaps you are wealthy and successful, and people are constantly asking things of you, but no one ever thinks of you first or asks what you need. Maybe you have experienced bad breaks all your life. You have been orphaned, homeless, and now sick in your body, and you feel as though you cannot get a break in life and bitterness and insecurity have become your daily food. What do you do? Where do you turn? Where did Michal turn?

Consider this prompt, and grab a notebook to journal your thoughts.

Has your hurt ever manifested itself as hate? Who or what do you turn to when you are hurt and angry: the bottle, pills, or a person you know you should stay away from?

9.

I CAN'T SEE GOD
FOR THE PAIN IN ME

e know Michal knew of God because her father had worshipped God until he became entangled with self-idolatry and jealousy. She also knew about God and what He could do by watching David defeat the Philistines again and again. David loved God with all his heart, openly, sang praises to God, and was known as a man of God. Michal, however, did not see the God that her father and David served in a positive light because of the way they treated her. Michal was repeatedly mistreated by those who claimed to serve a deity that was good, kind, and loving, and she could not understand how such a God could allow men to mistreat her.

Have you ever met someone who claimed to fear God, and yet was able to treat you like garbage? Have you been the person who tried to tell others about the great God you serve, but they cannot get past some terrible thing you did in the past? That is where Michal was stuck, in the place of conflating human behavior with God's nature. They are not one and the same, but they are often seen as the same when we focus on humanity.

Michal did not try to get to know God for herself, she just turned to her safe place of bitterness. Bitterness can become comfortable when you have lived with it and in it for so long. What do you do when a person who is loved by God is also your monster? You focus on their flawed humanity instead of on God's divinity. Michal knew about God, but did she have a personal experience with Him? Or did she rather allow her mind to focus on the humanity of two men, her father and David, and miss out on her deliverance by God because she was holding onto pain and bitterness?

Michal may have conflated David's anointing and his humanity in her mind. She did not see that human flesh will always fail us and that God is the only lover who will never leave us nor forsake us. Michal told David that he was ridiculous because of the way he was showing off for the women in town and that he was not behaving as a king should. She was, in a way, reminding him that he was not of noble birth, insinuating that if he was, he would have known that his behavior in front of his subjects was unbecoming of a king.

Michal spoke to King David out of her pain instead of speaking from her promise. Are you forsaking your promise for your pain? Are you holding onto trauma from your childhood that is sucking the life out of you? Are you using meanness as a shield of protection for your heart? Michal did just that, and she therefore was known to be mean, angry, and hateful.

Other biblical characters responded differently to negative circumstances. There were two brothers in the Bible, Jacob and Esau, and Jacob was something else. He was a swindler. You know that family member who is always trying to get away with this and that, the one always asking for money and never repaying? That was Jacob, the trickster. Esau, his brother, always tried to do the right thing, but Jacob was spoiled because he was the one his mother favored, and she always covered for him.

Esau hated Jacob so much for his tricky ways that he wanted to kill him in his anger. He vowed to kill him once their father died. Esau was vexed by the thought of his brother, Jacob, for a long time, but eventually, he decided to break that pain, and the yoke of heaviness fell from his heart and mind: he was mentally free.

It was not that he excused Jacob for what he did, but that he was able to focus on his own future and to move past his pain to focus on his purpose. He became wealthy and mentally free, and when he finally saw Jacob after some years, he was able to have genuine love and concern for his brother. Leaving the pain behind is not for the sake of the person who caused you the pain. You are not letting them off the hook, you are freeing yourself from the slow death of bitterness.

Michal's bitterness cost her everything. She did not give birth to any children, which, in biblical days, was devastating. David wanted nothing more to do with Michal. She was **dying in plain sight!** As you read through Michal's experience, I do not begin to excuse her behavior or to make the wrongs she committed right. I am not making excuses for anyone who allows bitterness to rule their life. My challenge is that you try to see past a person's bitterness and insecurity to their pain and humanity. They may need a little understanding and true healing down in their innermost being. Even if you cannot be in their presence because they have made it impossible to do so, ask God to touch them in their deepest pain and heal their heart, mind, and soul.

Some of you reading this book may be those who have allowed bitterness and insecurity to be your guide, your companion, and your only friends. People may gossip about you and look at you with judgmental glances, without knowledge of or regard for your personal and private pain. You have a choice to allow those glances, words, and thoughts of others, along with your own self-loathing and pain to keep you in bitterness, or to be better, healed, and whole. Figuring out how to heal is for you and not for those who hurt you. Stop speaking from your pain and choose to speak from your promise!

Consider this prompt, and grab a notebook to journal your thoughts.

What pain are you holding onto? What lie has a hold on your mind? Are you going through life speaking from your pain or your promise? Do you realize your life has purpose?

10.
A MATTER OF BATHSHEBA: THE VIXEN

et's start with some background and the first way Bathsheba is sometimes viewed, as a vixen. Her father's name was Eliam, an elite man in King David's service, and it is purported that her grandfather was Ahithophel, a wise man who counseled King David, which would make Bathsheba of noble birth.

Bathsheba was David's eighth and final wife. When people speak about her, she is often described in one of two ways: Bathsheba is described either as the victim of rape or as a vixen who beguiled King David and caused him to sin. Everyone reading this book probably has experienced being shamed because of something that has happened to you or something that you have done, or you know someone who has had that experience. Even in a house of worship, which should be a safe place, the spiritual hospital where you go to get your wounds tended when you are hurt, can sometimes feel like the most unsafe place to be when something in your life goes wrong. People tend to judge others' situations from the outside without knowing what happens on the inside. People are so focused on what they *think* is the sin that they often forget the hurt of the human being whom they are judging. Bathsheba's humanity is usually not the lens from which her story is told.

Let's look at Bathsheba's experience in the way that people speak about her as a vixen. Some say that she was a woman with a plan to seduce the King of Israel. She lusted for the power and the good things he could offer her. When the king was in town, everyone knew it. The king could not sneak into town undetected; he was the king! She knew King David liked to take nightly strolls, and after studying his habits, she discovered that he would sometimes walk on his rooftop at night. She devised a plan to set up her bath on her rooftop when her husband was away, as she knew David's rooftop overlooked hers. She slipped into her bath, and when King David appeared, she seductively gazed at him with coy glances. Once he saw her, he was hooked. She knew his reputation for loving the ladies, so she was confident that he would invite her to his palace.

King David did not disappoint, of course, as he sent a message for her to join him at the palace. She accepted his invitation, went over to the palace, and had sex with the king. She enjoyed her evening, and no one was the wiser until she missed her menstrual cycle. Panic set in; she knew that she could not claim that the pregnancy was from her husband, since he was away at war. In horror, she sent a message to King David to ask, "What will we do?" The king told her that he would take care of it.

Bathsheba knew that her pregnancy by another man would devastate her family in so many ways. Her father and husband would be disgraced by having a daughter and wife who had committed adultery. She was also in jeopardy of being stoned to death for her sin. Little did she know that when the king said that he would take care of the situation, he planned to kill her loving and faithful husband. Then in an instant, her husband was dead!

Bathsheba was then pregnant, alone, and married to the man with whom she had committed adultery, while everyone whispered about the king's new wife. She was called a vixen, bad for the king, an embarrassment to her family, and a murderer for having her husband killed to be with the king.

Have you ever seen people take a mistake you made and run with it? They act as though they have never done anything wrong, and as though you are the worst person on the planet. There is no place to run and nowhere to hide from such judgment when you are the wife of the king.

Though she dealt with backlash everywhere for the nine long months of her pregnancy, the one bright light was the day on which her beautiful baby boy was born. He looked handsome like his father but had her eyes. She was consumed with a love like she had never felt before. His warm, tiny hand gripped her finger, and he melted her heart from his first breath. He had ten little fingers and ten toes, and he was perfect!

Then two days later, he stopped feeding and developed a fever. None of the doctors could figure out what was wrong with her son. She was scared, David was pacing and refusing to eat, and the child was getting worse and worse. She was alone, with no one to keep her company while the doctors tried all they could think of to help the boy. She kept trying to nurse him, but he had no strength to eat and eventually, the inconceivable happened. At just seven days old, her beautiful baby boy was gone!

He died from no apparent cause. Bathsheba was devastated. She blamed herself for the child's death, alone, with no one to console her. She grieved and longed for her son until some time had passed, and though she still thought of him daily, she decided that she had to keep living and prospering to honor her son.

Consider this prompt, and grab a notebook to journal your thoughts.

Have you ever made a mistake with unintended consequences? Do people hold you to a mistake you made, and it seems like they will never let it go? How are you coping?

A MATTER OF BATHSHEBA: THE VICTIM

he second way Bathsheba is spoken of is as a victim. Bathsheba was living her life and minding her own business when one day, she went to her rooftop to bathe. During that time of the year, especially during times of war, kings usually went with their armies to battle their enemies. However, King David was at home in his palace while his soldiers were off fighting.

According to historic Jewish customs, bathing had various meanings: one might bathe to cleanse oneself, or one might practice ceremonial bathing. Women practiced ceremonial bathing to signal the completion of their menstrual cycle or the end of blood flow after childbirth.

One evening, when King David would normally have been at war, he was on his rooftop getting some fresh air. He spotted Bathsheba bathing and inquired who she was. Remember, her father was in his service, so he knew that she was of noble birth once he had learned her name. When he was told who her husband was, King David also knew him to be one of his mighty soldiers who was away fighting in a war for Israel and for his king. Bathsheba's husband's name was Uriah the Hittite, an honorable and loyal man.

King David summoned Bathsheba to his palace and raped her. He then sent her away after the deed was done. He was the king, the person with all the power, the boss of her husband and her father, and the king they admired.

How would Bathsheba be safe if she screamed or protested the king's advances? What about her father's and husband's safety? Who do you run to when the most influential person you know is your abuser? Where do you turn when the people who should keep you safe are the very people abusing you? Who would believe you if you told someone? What do you do when your boss steals your idea and presents it as their own? What recourse do you have? What do you do when your parent or your parents' closest friend molests you and threatens to turn the situation on you? Who do you turn to when the priest, the deacon, or the pastor betrays their sacred trust? Who do you turn to when the whole world praises your abuser?

That is where Bathsheba found herself, raped, alone, afraid, and ashamed. She could not tell her father that his boss and king had raped her. She did not want to put her father's life in jeopardy. She couldn't tell her husband, who worshipped the ground King David walked on. What if he didn't believe her? Where would she go? She had no one to confide in, so she suffered in silence.

There is no mention of anyone aiding Bathsheba after her rape. There was no therapy, no friends to trust—or maybe there was someone she had thought to be a friend and confidant, but instead of comforting Bathsheba, they lied about her compounding the situation.

Not only was Bathsheba the victim of a malicious rape, but then the rapist plotted and succeeded in killing her loyal and faithful husband. She was left alone and afraid. **Dying in plain sight!**

David is later scolded by Nathan the prophet and punished by God through the death of Bathsheba's son, but no one speaks of Bathsheba's pain; they only pity David, because he was distraught about his son's looming death. People often talk about the incident as adultery, but adultery is a voluntary act between people where at least one of those people is married. How do you reject the king?

The rape also resulted in a pregnancy, and after carrying the baby to term and delivering her son, Bathsheba's child died. The death of a child is an unimaginable pain! The thought of a child may have been the only solace that kept her from giving up on life, and then the child died.

No one talks about the pain she may have endured from losing her precious son. Or maybe she was relieved that the child born from rape did not survive. That may sound crass to many, but if you have experienced sexual assault, you understand the trauma and the lingering impact it can have. No one knows how Bathsheba felt because her perspective is not included in the story and often it seems that no one cares.

Many people cast aside Bathsheba's trauma and pain and focus on the heartache that King David felt for his dying son. David was surely heartbroken about his son's illness and subsequent death, but why was Bathsheba forgotten in that moment? Have you ever been wronged, betrayed, broken, and then cast aside, as if your pain was somehow less important? Have you ever felt that no one cares about the agony you've endured? Though some people do believe that Bathsheba was raped, her trauma is not often examined or highlighted in deeper ways. No one discusses how she may have engaged in victim blaming.

"Why did I go on that roof? What was I thinking? How do I protect my father and my husband? Who will believe me? Should I have told the King, NO? WHAT AM I GOING TO DO NOW?!"

WHEN PEOPLE ARE BELOVED as King David was and is, sometimes their human flaws are thrust behind their larger-than-life persona, and it even becomes taboo to talk honestly about their whole story or any wrong they may have done. There is an unconscious cover-up to protect their name. That cover-up becomes turned on the victim, the abused, the raped, the one who does not receive the care and compassion that someone who has experienced trauma should receive. Maybe it is an unconscious way of trying to protect God, but God needs no protection from the truth. The truth can be told, and healing can begin. Living in the shadow of trauma and defeat does not have to be the end of your story.

Consider this prompt, and grab a notebook to journal your thoughts.

Have you ever been blamed for something you didn't do? How did you handle the lie and the pain it caused you? Even though you can never chase down a lie and shouldn't bother trying, the lie, the looks, and whispers can have a lasting sting if you let them. Are you suffering in silence?

12.
MICHAL:
POOR BATHSHEBA

JOURNAL SEVEN

DEAR DIARY, David is at it again, destroying lives. He raped Bathsheba. I know people do not believe her, but that is because they do not know David like I do. Yes, he is a God-fearing man, but he is also human. How is Bathsheba getting all the blame? How did I get all the blame? Why does he get to do whatever he wants while we seem to be required to suffer in silence? You know when someone with clout or power of some kind is involved, people pick sides with them, even if they must lie to align themselves with the most despicable. How is Bathsheba so silent! I recently heard the term "gaslighting," which is when people try to make you think you don't know what you know and you don't remember things how you know they are to be, and they try to make you look like you are crazy for speaking your truth. This whole town is gaslighting Bathsheba, and I do not understand why she won't speak up for herself!

BATHSHEBA IS IN THE PALACE alone without a friend. She knows the king only married her to save himself from being stoned, because if anyone found out what really happened, he could be punished. Even if they do not believe Bathsheba, adultery is a sin, and David can be punished by death. Her family has not come to visit, and I know she is wondering what they are thinking of her. She finally birthed her son, and I know she had to be happy to have at least one person who loved her and needed her every day. I know I would if I had a child. Her son kept her company for a few days, and then the unthinkable happened. Her beloved son got sick.

Everyone is focused on consoling the king and making sure all his needs are met, as usual, but no one cares about Bathsheba! She is in the palace with all the kings' loyal subjects and wives who probably think she weaseled her way in, so no one will care to check on her and consider the broken heart of a mother whose child was dying in her arms. Remember I lived that life way before she did, and I know these people. The people of the town start talking and saying things like, "That is what she gets! The King deserves better." "She is nothing but a home wrecker!" No matter what anyone does, no one deserves to see their child die.

Bathsheba is a mother who must figure out how to get up every day after the death of her child. A mother's love is an unexplainable phenomenon. Mothers care for their children in ways that often make no sense to others. I learned that from watching my sister and her children. Even if a child has stolen from them, cursed them, and ignored them in their time of need, a mother will still love their child. Mothers love their children enough to go without eating to make sure they can eat. Some mothers give their children up so that they can have a better life, instead of making them suffer and go without, like Moses' mom did. David RUINS lives!

Consider this prompt, and grab a notebook to journal your thoughts.

Do you ever feel unseen, unheard, and uncared for? Do you see trauma in every situation now? Does your support even look angry?

13.
A MOTHER'S LOVE

mother's love is a mysterious thing. Mary the mother of Jesus stayed and watched Jesus while he was being crucified on the cross. Watching her child suffer being nailed to a piece of wood while she was powerless to do anything about it. People were screaming horrific insults while her baby was dying, yet she stayed so He did not die alone. Mary knew that He was destined for great things at an early age, but I am sure that she could not have imagined the path that greatness would take Him. She did not turn away and say, "I cannot watch my baby go through this," she stayed until He breathed His last breath. Mary stayed to let her son know, as God lets us know, "I will never leave you nor forsake you" (Hebrews 13:5).

Another mother who loved her sons beyond the point of death was a woman named Rizpah, one of King Saul's concubines. She was accused of having sex with

Abner, King Saul's cousin after the King's death. No one knows if it was consensual or not, or even if it occurred. Accusations sometimes take on a life of their own, and people never bother to find the truth.

Rizpah had two sons by King Saul. Because King Saul had sinned by the unrighteous killing of the Gibeonites, David asked them what they wanted in return to remove the sin from Israel. The Gibeonites asked him to kill some of King Saul's sons.

Rizpah's sons were two of the seven sons of King Saul killed by hanging. Again, like Mary, the mother of Jesus, Rizpah was powerless to stop it. She sat with her son's dead bodies, guarding them against scavenger birds and wild animals that would come to devour their rotting flesh. Some scholars say that she did this for four to six months. After hearing about what Rizpah was doing to guard her sons' bodies, King David allowed the bodies to be taken down and buried in King Saul's family grave-yard. Rizpah kept loving her sons even after their death and persisted until they were placed in the royal burial place. A mother's love transcends death.

You may feel like you do not understand a mother's love because your mother was not motherly, or she left you, or she was abusive, and I can understand that because of my experience with my biological father. When preachers would say, "God cares for you like your earthly father cares for you," I could not make a connection with that idea. My father was not a nurturing father, a giving father, or a present father. I did not connect with that kind of father, though that changed later in life with my bonus father, and then even later in life when my biological father and I reconnected a few years before his death.

It was not until his passing that I learned about a lot of his pain and the rejection he had suffered, which allowed me to understand more of his personal story. Not everyone will get to learn why their parent rejected or left them. They may never understand that their parent was flawed and marred by their own experiences, or that they did not have anything to give to anyone else, as I didn't for most of my life. Until that time, I struggled to see God as a Father, though I was able to connect with Him as a true friend. God taught me what it meant for Him to be my Father when I let go of the pain of the past.

Consider this prompt, and grab a notebook to journal your thoughts.

Have you experienced a mother's love, or are you still yearning for that mysterious kind of love? Do you know God in an intimate, personal way, as a father or a friend, or is the only thing you know about God from another's human perspective?

CAN YOU REALLY UNDERSTAND BATHSHEBA?

onsider the pain Bathsheba was experiencing, regardless of what you may think of her situation. What do you do when your life is shattered in an instant and no person comes to your defense? You must turn to God. Whether you think that Bathsheba was the victim or the vixen, you must understand that her past did not define her future. God protects His people from the enemy of our souls and often protects us from ourselves. He does that by drawing us closer to His love, which is a perfect and everlasting love. It is not like human love that is here today and gone tomorrow. God's love stays with us in the good and bad times, giving us a supernatural comfort that only God can give.

We cannot trust our own thoughts during tough times when we are feeling down on ourselves and listening to the gossip of the world. We must realize and believe that our heavenly Father loves us with a perfect love that cannot be diminished by what happens to us or even by what we do. Bathsheba did not allow her situation to make her heart grow cold and bitter. She was blessed with a second son, Solomon. He eventually became the next King of Israel after his father, David. A king has ultimate power in their kingdom, and the person that sits on the right side of a king is symbolically the second most important person in the kingdom.

One day Bathsheba went to talk to her son, the king. When she arrived, King Solomon not only bowed to his mother, but also told his people to get a chair and have his mother sit on his right side.

Bathsheba has been talked about, cast down, lied about, and had her name maligned from generation to generation. She was raped and forsaken, yet she did not allow her circumstances to become bitter roots that would bind her. She allowed the pain that she had survived to strengthen her so she could advocate for her son to be king and for her place beside his throne.

Bathsheba wrote a proverbial thank you letter to all those who counted her as unworthy by living her best life, fighting through her pain, and finding peace within, through God. Though she was **dying in plain sight**, she was also dying to the opinions of other people. She learned to ignore the naysayers and focus on the Giver of

Life and His plan for her. She was dying to the negative voices in her head that tried to tell her that she was not enough. She learned to **live, not to die!**

Consider this prompt, and grab a notebook to journal your thoughts.

You can fight through the pain to see your promise. Are you willing to take a step out of your dark places and into God's light?

15.
BATHSHEBA:
MY DEAR SISTER MICHAL

ichal, I consider you to be a big sister. I know that we were not able to be around each other, but I know that you have a beautiful fire inside of you that was never nourished. I thank you for being one of the only people who has ever cared to SEE me. You did not jump on the "hate Bathsheba" band wagon, and I truly love you for that. I have never spoken publicly because I do not believe that you can chase a lie. It is fruitless: as I was told as a child, "chasing a lie is like a dog chasing its tail, it will never catch it."

Despite what happened with David, thankfully, I had a good foundation of love in my family: love that shared, love that gave, love that talked openly and honestly about life, which prepared me, in a way, for life's challenges. The first lesson I learned growing up was to love myself and to know who I am, a child of God. People will speak of things of which they do not know *because* they do not know. I laugh because it seems so odd when you say it, but it really is true. People will say you are snooty if you do not tell them all your business. People will say you are wrong without knowing all the facts. People will doubt your integrity without ever uttering one word to you or without having any relationship with you at all, and sometimes those who do have a relationship with you will judge you unfairly. You may not have known that they were secretly envious or jealous of you, or that their low self-esteem was the catalyst for their envy and spite. However, to love yourself, which means trying to live a life of truth, even if you get it wrong from time to time, is what is essential.

I learned to love the person that God made me to be in all of who I am. God made me wonderfully, and people may try their best to tear me down from the outside in and the inside out, but when you have a good foundation of loving yourself, they can only go so far. Now, I am not a saint and I have let people affect me in ways in which I wish I had not, but I always remember that God made me, that I belong to God, and that I must block out the haters. Some people who I thought would have stuck by me during the David scandal did not, and some of my closest "friends" were the ones who slandered me the most. I was not heard or seen and felt dejected, but I knew, and still know, that God loves me.

David may not have thought of his actions as rape at that time, but I believe that that changed many years later. You see, his beautiful teenage daughter, Tamar, was raped by her half-brother Amnon. As you know, they are his children by his other wives. David found out about the rape, and though he was angry over it, he did nothing to his son. David and I never spoke of it, but I believe he realized in that moment what he had done to me, and the pain and trauma I had endured. David grappled with how he could chastise his son when he had done the same terrible deed to me all those years ago. His guilt and shame paralyzed him and prevented him from doing anything about the situation, which caused a domino effect and again, as you know, his other son, Absalom, took matters in his own hands and killed Amnon.

Michal, what you don't understand is that healing myself and finding a way to move into my future in a healthy manner does not mean that I excused David's behavior at all. It means that I cannot allow someone else's wrong to imprison my mind, heart, and soul while they live free. If I did that, it would mean that I allowed them to continue to abuse me and to steal my future and my destiny of greatness. I had to realize that I was worth more than what happened to me, and I had to focus on the great things in store for me.

You and I have been around David long enough to have learned some survival skills from him. Even if you still feel like he is your enemy, use the tools of your enemy to live. Remember that when David thought he had lost everything, he encouraged himself in the Lord. Well, I use that very tool. I encouraged myself and continue to encourage myself in the Lord! How do you think I survived my son's death, or the constant vitriol I receive from people? First, I remember I am a child of the Most High God, I know I am wonderfully made in His sight, I pray all the time, and I know how to encourage myself in the Lord when times get tough. I learned that from watching David. You can learn from anyone; you just have to learn how to eat the meat and throw away the bones. Even if I wanted to give up on myself, I couldn't, because my son needed me if he was going to be a good king. I do not mean that I ignored all that I was going through to focus on him, although I dedicated my life to his welfare. What I mean is that I had to make sure that I was whole, spiritually, physically, and mentally, because I cannot do anything for anyone while I am broken down, living my life through the looking glass of pity.

I am not writing you this letter to shame you in any way. I write you this letter, my sister, to say that I want you to LIVE! You have been *dying in plain sight* for long enough. It is time for you to let go of your past childhood trauma, the pain of a bad marriage, fear, jealousy, envy, and yes, that dirty, old dog of bitterness that will destroy your heart, mind, and soul. Your sister Merab is gone now, and her children need you, but they don't need you in broken pieces, they need you whole. Speak life to yourself. Start speaking those positive things about yourself that you wished you heard from your father and from David. Tell yourself that you are intelligent, beautiful, and worthy of the great things that life has to offer. Know that you are loved by God and that you have the love of God in you to share with others. I have more things to share with you about my life and experiences that may help you understand me and my choices, but I want you to have some time to think about what I have shared already. I do not want to overwhelm your mind. I just want you to heal your broken heart.

Dying in plain sight is <u>NOT</u> your destiny, **my sister, so LIVE!**

Consider this prompt, and grab a notebook to journal your thoughts.

Are you ready to dare to love YOU? Speak life to yourself because you are wonderfully made!

16.
CHOOSE LIFE!

ike Bathsheba, you may have been labeled the problem, even though you were the abused. I know a wonderful woman who endured physical abuse, and the people who could have helped her, shielded her, and guided her to self-love, instead chose to tell her that the abuse was her fault because she was obviously not a good wife. She had to figure out how to navigate life mentally, emotionally, and spiritually through and from her trauma, often silently and alone. She chose to have a relationship with God and to be healed from within by His grace and power. She did not stay bitter, she chose better: She chose the Great I AM, the God who made Heaven and earth!

Like this woman, if anyone should have been bitter, it was Bathsheba, but she chose a different route than Michal. Her grandfather was Ahithophel, who counseled

King David before supporting the king's son Absalom in a coup against his father. Scholars surmise he backed Absalom because King David raped his granddaughter Bathsheba. He was bitter, and he allowed that bitterness to grow and to fester in his mind and heart. He was unsuccessful in his attempts to counsel Absalom against King David and subsequently committed suicide when his advice was not taken. King David's actions not only negatively impacted Bathsheba, but they had a ripple effect on her entire family. Her husband was killed, her grandfather committed suicide, and her name was and is still maligned, but Bathsheba did not allow those things to stop her. She did not take the road of bitterness as her grandfather did. She chose **life**!

Bathsheba went to a dying King David to make sure that her son was appointed as the next king upon David's death. She went without being called by the king, which could have ended in her death, but she knew that she had endured much worse. She had built up an inner strength and trust in God that gave her the boldness she needed to save her son. Bathsheba chose her son; she chose **life**! Michal turned to her friends, Bitterness and Insecurity, while Bathsheba turned to her friends, Grace and Mercy. Bathsheba sat on the right hand of her son, which denotes power, authority, and a special place of honor. Though people gossiped about Bathsheba, it didn't make her any less blessed. Your reactions do not define my relevance. Do not see yourself through the filters of others. What people think about you cannot stop God's elevation for you. See yourself through the lens of God, who said you are *wonderfully* made!

Now, I know most people feel that Michal was punished for the rest of her life because she could not physically have any children, but many scholars believe that she raised her sister's four children after her passing. We know that there are many ways to be a parent, and birthing children is not the only way. It is possible that Michal decided to free herself from her bitterness and was then able to raise her sister's children with the love and joy she found in God. Do not give up on others, and do not give up on yourself. Most people's lives are neither all good nor all bad. We have a mixed bag of experiences throughout our lifetime. It is possible to have bitter seasons when you feel like Michal as well as seasons when you feel like an overcomer, like Bathsheba. The key is to recognize when your mind and heart are leaning toward bitterness and pray your way out of the dark places of your mind. Instead of dying in plain sight, choose to **live**!

Consider this prompt, and grab a notebook to journal your thoughts.

In what ways will you now choose life and live more abundantly?

Volume One
JOURNAL PAGES

ournaling can help you process your thoughts, feelings, and say things you may not feel comfortable saying to anyone. If you're new to journaling, consider Michal's reflections. The prompts and pages that follow are for your thoughts. Write a reflection (or draw, doodle, create in your way) after reading each chapter. You may need time to process your thoughts and feelings after a chapter, so feel free to go back and journal after you have had time to process. There is no right or wrong time or way to journal.

CHAPTER 1 JOURNAL PROMPT

Take a few moments to assess how you are feeling after reading chapter one. Describe what memories come to mind about your life, whether painful or pleasant, and jot down your thoughts. Who were your confidants as a child? How did you cope with childhood trauma/issues?

_____

_____

_____

_____

_____

_____

_____

_____

_____

_____

_____

_____

_____

CHAPTER 2 JOURNAL PROMPT

What are the thoughts that come to mind about yourself? Are they uplifting thoughts or self-deprecating thoughts? Take a deep look into the recesses of your heart and mind and journal about your thoughts of you. Consider the relationship you had with your parents or caregivers. How did those relationships contribute to your thoughts about yourself?

_____

_____

_____

_____

_____

_____

_____

_____

_____

_____

_____

_____

_____

_____

CHAPTER 3 JOURNAL PROMPT

How has the way you see yourself impacted your relationships with family, friends, coworkers, and acquaintances? Do you have healthy relationships, or do you struggle to maintain nourishing relationships? What self-sabotaging threats have you created within your mind?

_____

_____

_____

_____

_____

_____

_____

_____

_____

_____

_____

_____

_____

_____

CHAPTER 4 JOURNAL PROMPT

Have you ever loved someone who did not love you back equally? Have you ever been disappointed by someone's actions—like Michal was over her father's hatred of her husband—and you felt stuck in the middle? How did that feel? What choices did you feel you had?

_____

_____

_____

_____

_____

_____

_____

_____

_____

_____

_____

_____

_____

_____

_____

CHAPTER 5 JOURNAL PROMPT

How do you deal with thoughts of comparison that may pop into your mind? Comparisons to other people's beauty, intellect, or wealth? What do you do to rid your mind of negative comparison thoughts, or do you embrace them and let them grow? If you feel broken, can you recognize where and when the brokenness was birthed?

_____

_____

_____

_____

_____

_____

_____

_____

_____

_____

_____

_____

_____

_____

_____

CHAPTER 6 JOURNAL PROMPT

How do you deal with the unthankful or ungrateful people in your life? Do you continue to cater to them to keep them nearby? Do you block everyone out of your life so as not to feel the hurt that you have experienced by the few ungrateful people you have encountered?

_____

_____

_____

_____

_____

_____

_____

_____

_____

_____

_____

_____

_____

_____

CHAPTER 7 JOURNAL PROMPT

Are you always the caregiver and never the one being cared for? What do you do to put yourself first? What self-care regimen have you established for your life? Are you feeding on a diet of bitterness and insecurity?

_____

_____

_____

_____

_____

_____

_____

_____

_____

_____

_____

_____

_____

_____

_____

_____

_____

_____

_____

_____

_____

_____

_____

_____

_____

_____

_____

_____

_____

_____

_____

_____

_____

_____

_____

_____

_____

CHAPTER 8 JOURNAL PROMPT

Has your hurt ever manifested itself as hate? Who or what do you turn to when you are hurt and angry: the bottle, pills, or a person you know you should stay away from?

_____

_____

_____

_____

_____

_____

_____

_____

_____

_____

_____

_____

_____

_____

_____

_____

DR. ROYCE M. CARPENTER

_____

_____

_____

_____

_____

_____

_____

_____

_____

_____

_____

_____

_____

_____

_____

_____

_____

_____

_____

_____

_____

CHAPTER 9 JOURNAL PROMPT

What pain are you holding onto? What lie has a hold on your mind? Are you going through life speaking from your pain or your promise? Do you realize your life has purpose?

_____

_____

_____

_____

_____

_____

_____

_____

_____

_____

_____

_____

_____

_____

_____

_____

DR. ROYCE M. CARPENTER

_____

_____

_____

_____

_____

_____

_____

_____

_____

_____

_____

_____

_____

_____

_____

_____

_____

_____

_____

_____

_____

CHAPTER **10** JOURNAL PROMPT

Have you ever made a mistake with unintended conse-quences? Do people hold you to a mistake you made, and it seems like they will never let it go? How are you coping?

_____

_____

_____

_____

_____

_____

_____

_____

_____

_____

_____

_____

_____

_____

_____

_____

_____

_____

_____

_____

_____

_____

_____

_____

_____

_____

_____

_____

_____

_____

_____

_____

_____

_____

CHAPTER 11 JOURNAL PROMPT

Have you ever been blamed for something you didn't do? How did you handle the lie and the pain it caused you? Even though you can never chase down a lie and shouldn't bother trying, the lie, the looks, and whispers can have a lasting sting if you let them. Are you suffering in silence?

_____

_____

_____

_____

_____

_____

_____

_____

_____

_____

_____

_____

_____

_____

_____

CHAPTER **12** JOURNAL PROMPT

Do you ever feel unseen, unheard, and uncared for? Do you see trauma in every situation now? Does your support even look angry?

_____

_____

_____

_____

_____

_____

_____

_____

_____

_____

_____

_____

_____

_____

_____

_____

CHAPTER 13 JOURNAL PROMPT

Have you experienced a mother's love, or are you still yearning for that mysterious kind of love? Do you know God in an intimate, personal way, as a father or a friend, or is the only thing you know about God from another's human perspective?

_____

_____

_____

_____

_____

_____

_____

_____

_____

_____

_____

_____

_____

_____

_____

_____

_____

_____

_____

_____

_____

_____

_____

_____

_____

_____

_____

_____

_____

_____

_____

_____

_____

_____

CHAPTER **14** JOURNAL PROMPT

You can fight through the pain to see your promise. Are you willing to take a step out of your dark places and into God's light?

_____

_____

_____

_____

_____

_____

_____

_____

_____

_____

_____

_____

_____

_____

_____

_____

_____

CHAPTER **15** JOURNAL PROMPT

Are you ready to dare to love YOU? Speak life to yourself because you are wonderfully made!

_____

_____

_____

_____

_____

_____

_____

_____

_____

_____

_____

_____

_____

_____

_____

_____

_____

_____

CHAPTER 16 JOURNAL PROMPT

In what ways will you now choose life and live more abundantly?

_____

_____

_____

_____

_____

_____

_____

_____

_____

_____

_____

_____

_____

_____

_____

_____

_____

ACKNOWLEDGMENTS

hank you, Jesus, my Lord and Savior, for carrying me through tests and trials and knowing that I would bend but not break even when I felt broken. Thank you to everyone who survived and thrived all that life threw at them to be an example of resilience and strength for others to emulate.

To my parents, Chris and Valerie Washington, thank you for always being there for me with love and sound advice. My dear children, Anthony, Devin, Nia, and Malik, I am blessed to call you my true love, and thank you for encouraging me to keep reaching for my dreams. To my grandchildren, Aubrie, Zy'ion, Kaidyn, Nova, Aniyah, D.J., Moses, Aspen, and Avery, thank you for the joy and light you bring into my daily world. To my lifetime confidant, my sister, and best friend, Pamela Simmons, you have known me, your little sister, all my life, kept all my secrets, and shared childhood dreams that are coming to fruition. Thank you for being my loving big sister. Momma Peggy, what can I say about you and Papa John? You both saved me from myself as a teenager and never stopped showering me with everlasting love. Thank you. Auntie Lynda, you are a perfect example of what In-Law Love looks like, and I cannot thank you enough for loving not only your nephew but me, too, ever since I met you. To the only E. Melody Watkins who can get me together and love me all in the same sentence, lol, I love you.

Thank you to Dr. Sherman S. Watkins for being an impeccable example of excellence in everything he does, for loving God unreservedly and unapologetically, and for giving me a road map to learn how to study and know the truth for myself. Thank you to Dr. Billy Newman and Dr. Terrence Brooks for your keen insights and advice on this literary journey. You both selfishly gave your time and direction, and I pray many blessings for you. Thank you to Emily Hitchcock, Clair Fink, Katie Blatter for her brilliant editing, and the entire editing team at Columbus Publishing Lab, who aided my first literary work to fruition. To my fantastic illustrator, Aaron Richmond of Aphografx, thank you! You listened to my vision for the book cover and made my words come to life.

Finally, to the love of my life, Walter Carpenter, you have been by my side for nearly four decades, and I could not imagine a better partner, friend, husband, or lover than you. We have seen each other through good times and bad, ups and downs, joys and sorrows while raising children, seeing grandchildren grow, and everything in between. Thank you for telling me to go for it every time I want to take my career and education to the next level and go for things others may have said were impossible or inaccessible. You never wavered in your belief that I could achieve anything I set my mind to do. Thank you for being the only one who could handle me for these thirty-seven years, as the kids would say (big smile). Thank you for understanding the challenges I have faced with kindness and understanding, and for walking with me through the storms and not letting go. I love you to the moon and back!

ABOUT THE AUTHOR

r. Royce M. Carpenter is an Associate Professor, a life coach, cross-cultural mentoring trainer, and workshop presenter on cultural development, and leadership cultural competency for higher education institutions and for-profit and non-profit organizations. Carpenter's work includes teaching and facilitating courageous conversations necessary for students, educators, leaders, and communities to look outward and within. She says understanding oneself is imperative for self-realization, allowing for a better understanding of others' perspectives and their need for love and compassion.

Printed in the USA
CPSIA information can be obtained
at www.ICGtesting.com
CBHW030720140524
8433CB00001B/2

9 781633 379091